First Time
ANALOGIES

Written by Dianne Draze

Illustrated by Mary Lou Johnson

Published by Prufrock Press Inc.

ISBN-13: 978-1-59363-073-7

Questions regarding this book should be addressed to:
  Prufrock Press Inc.
  P.O. Box 8813
  Waco, TX 76714-8813
  800-998-2208

For more information about Prufrock Press products, visit our website
www.prufrock.com

Contents

Teaching Notes

What Is an Analogy?

An analogy is a comparison between two items. It points out the similarities or likenesses between things that might be different in all other respects. Analogies draw a parallel between the common characteristics of two things and cause us to think analytically about forms, usages, structures, and relationships.

In order to solve the analogy, students need to analyze the elements of the puzzle, define a relationship between two things, and then apply this relationship to two other things. As students look for new relationships, creative combinations, or untried similarities, they will be exercising flexible as well as critical thinking.

A typical analogy would look like the following:
① is to ❶ as ✧ is to ✦
→ is to ➡ as ✕ is to ✖
▲ is to ▼ as ⅋ is to ⅋
bark is to **dog** as **meow** is to **cat**
red is to **pink** as **purple** is to **mauve**.

About This Book

First Time Analogies is designed to introduce analogies to the pre-reader. All the analogies are pictorial or symbolic. In this way, young students can practice the same logical thinking skills that are usually introduced in verbal analogies.

This book is divided into four sections, each one presenting analogies with different formats and degrees of difficulty.

Relationships

The first section presents work on identifying relationships, because being able to identify the relationship between two things is a prerequisite to solving analogies. In the first section (lessons 1 - 4), students are given four pictures, three of which are related, and asked to select the one item that does not belong. You may want to discuss each exercise, asking students why they chose to eliminate the one item and how the other three are related. This strengthens not only their reasoning skills but also their ability to verbally explain their reasoning. In the second section (lessons 5 - 8) students are given one item and asked to select one other item that is related to it. Again, ask students to explain their reasoning. You may find that they are able to find a very logical relationship other than the one that is designated as the correct answer. The designated answer is probably the stronger of the two relationships, but you may want to reward good logical thinking even if it doesn't meet the "correct answer" test.

Analogies - Level 1 (one choice)

The first level of analogy exercises (lesson 9 - 18) presents two things that are related. It then presents a third picture and asks students to choose one thing (from three

items) so that it is related to the third picture in the same way that the first two pictures are related. An example would be:

(**coin** is to **piggy bank** as **card** is to **envelope**).

These activities present analogies based on group membership, usage, position and reversals, coloration, size, parts of a whole, dimension, and adding or subtracting details.

Analogies - Level 2 (two choices)

Each page in the second level (lessons 19 - 28) has the beginning of four analogies. For each analogy, pictures of two things that are related to each other are presented. On another page are picture blocks that students cut out and use to complete the analogies. For instance, to complete the analogies in lesson 19 (page 23) students would be given the answer blocks on the top of page 25. They would cut these pictures apart, arrange them in appropriate places to form analogies and then glue the pictures in place. Next to the pictures of hair and comb, they would glue pictures of a tooth and a toothbrush (*hair is to comb as tooth is to toothbrush*). It is advisable that students play around with the pictures before they glue any in place. Some of the analogies are more obvious; and if need, other, harder, analogies can be completed through a process of elimination. In some of the problems (ones showing group membership, for instance), the order in which the pictures are positioned does not matter. In other problems (size, for example) the order may be critical to forming a correct analogy.

Analogies - Level Three (matching four things)

The last section of this book (lesson 29 - 37) gives sixteen pictures and asks students to cut out the pictures, arrange them into four valid analogies and paste them on another piece of paper. While this involves processing a lot of information, if students have worked through the previous exercises so they understand the concepts of relationships and analogies, this should be a challenging but not impossible task. As before, students should look for obvious pairings first and move all pictures into position before gluing any of them to the paper. If they need additional help to get started, you may wish to give them hints about one or two pairs. Since the analogies are unstructured, the order in which students chose to express the analogies may vary. They can form the analogy:
shovel is to spoon as bucket is to bowl or
shovel is to bucket as spoon is to bowl.
Both would be correct, so allow some flexibility in what you accept as a correct answer.

Name _____

Circle the one thing in each row that does not belong.

1.

2.

3.

4.

Name _____

Circle the one thing in each row that does not belong.

1.

2.

3.

4.

© Prufrock Press Inc. — First Time Analogies

Name _____

Circle the one thing in each row that does not belong.

1.

2.

3.

4.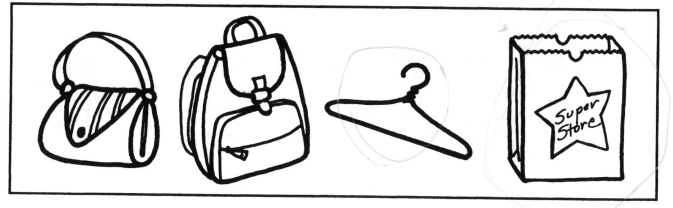

Name _____

Circle the one thing in each row that does not belong.

1.

2.

3.

4.

8

Name _____

Circle the picture that has something in common with the first picture.

1.    a.   b.    c.

2.    a.    b.   c.

3.    a.    b.    c.

4.   a.    b.    c.

5.    a.    b.   c.

Name _____

Circle the picture that has something in common with the first picture.

1.    a.    b.    c.

2.    a.    b.    c.

3.    a.    b.    c.

4.    a.    b.    c.

5.    a.   b.   c.

Name _____

Circle the picture that has something in common with the first picture.

1.    a. 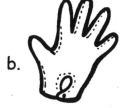   b.    c.

2.    a.   b.   c.

3.    a.    b.   c.

4.   a.   b.    c.

5.    a.    b.   c.

Name _____

Circle the picture that has something in common with the first picture.

1.    a.    b.    c.

2.    a.    b.    c.

3.    a.    b.    c.

4.    a.    b.    c.

5.    a.    b.    c.

Name _____

Circle the picture that is related to the thing in the small box in the same way the two things in the large box are related.

1. 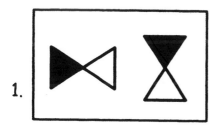  is like   a.   b.   c.

2.  is like   a.   b.   c.

3.   is like   a.    b.   c.

4.   is like   a.    b.   c.

5.   is like   a.   b.   c.

Name _____

Circle the picture that is related to the thing in the small box in the same way the two things in the large box are related.

1.   is like a.  b. 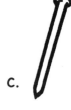 c.

2.   is like a.  b.  c.

3. 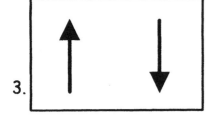  is like a.   b.   c.

4. 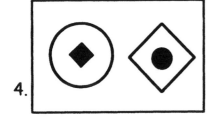 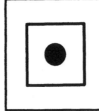 is like a.   b.   c.

5.   is like a. 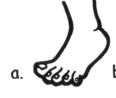 b. 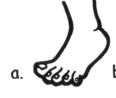 c.

Name _____

Circle the picture that is related to the thing in the small box in the same way the two things in the large box are related.

1.   is like   a.   b.   c.

2. 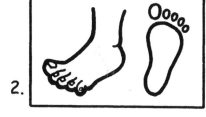  is like   a.   b.   c.

3. 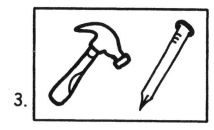  is like   a.   b.    c.

4.   is like   a.   b. 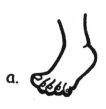   c.

5. 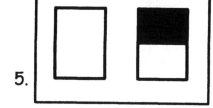 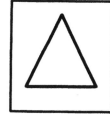 is like   a.   b.    c.

Name _____

Circle the picture that is related to the thing in the small box in the same way the two things in the large box are related.

1. 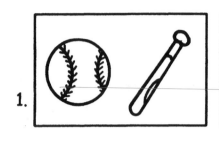  is like a.  b.  c.

2.   is like a. 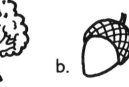 b. c.

3. 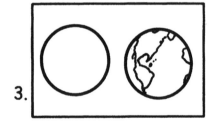  is like a. b.  c.

4. 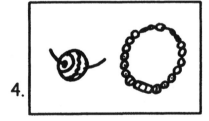  is like a. 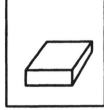 b. 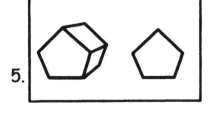 c.

5. 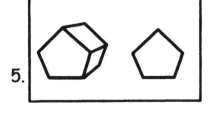 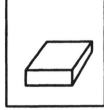 is like a. b. c.

Name _____

Circle the picture that is related to the thing in the small box in the same way the two things in the large box are related.

1.   is like a.  b.  c.

2. 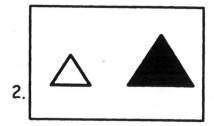 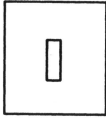 is like a. b. c.

3. 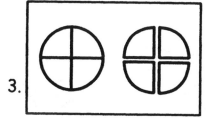  is like a. b. 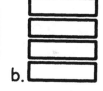 c.

4.  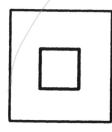 is like a.  b. c.

5.  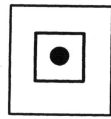 is like a. b. c.

Name _____

Circle the picture that is related to the thing in the small box in the same way the two things in the large box are related.

1.   is like a. b.  c.

2. 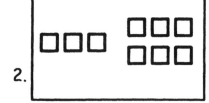  is like a.  b.  c.

3.   is like a. b. c.

4.   is like a. b.  c.

5.  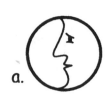 is like a. b. c.

Name _____

Circle the picture that is related to the thing in the small box in the same way the two things in the large box are related.

1. 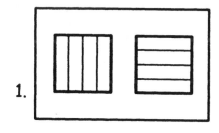  is like a. b. c.

2.   is like a.  b. c.

3. 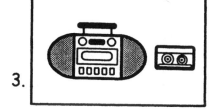  is like a. b. c.

4.   is like a. 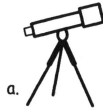 b. c.

5.   is like a. b. c.

Name _____

Circle the picture that is related to the thing in the small box in the same way the two things in the large box are related.

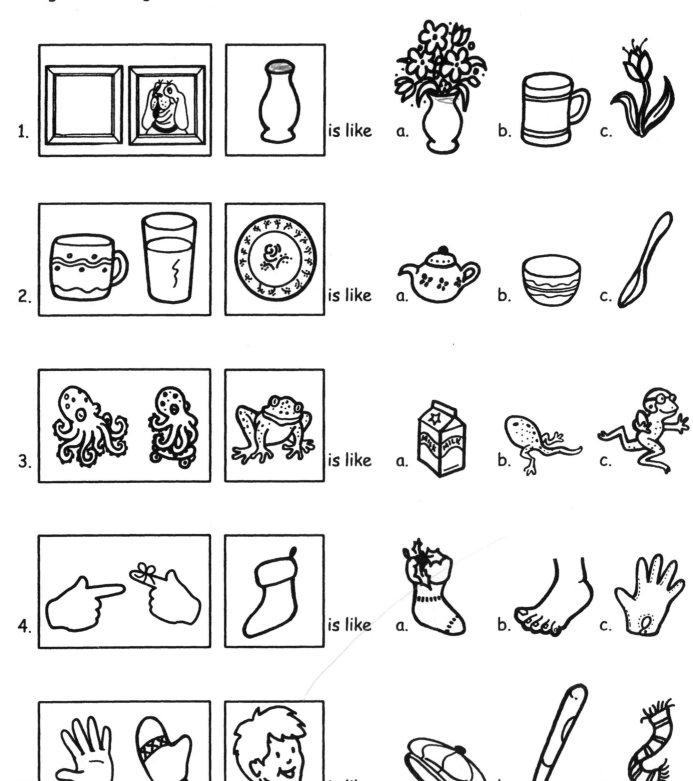

Name _____

Circle the picture that is related to the thing in the small box in the same way the two things in the large box are related.

1.  is like a. b. c.

2. 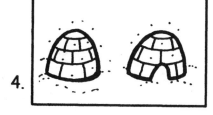  is like a. b. c.

3.   is like a. b. c.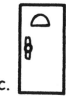

4.   is like a.  b. c.

5. **B T** **3** is like a. **8** b. **M** c. **:**

Name _____

Circle the picture that is related to the thing in the small box in the same way the two things in the large box are related.

1.   is like a. b.  c.

2. 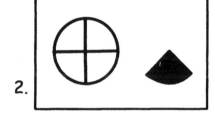  is like a. 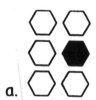 b. c.

3.   is like a. b.  c.

4.   is like a.  b.  c.

5.  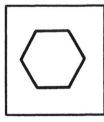 is like a. b. c.

Name _____

Cut out the pictures on page 25 and glue them in the second box so that these two things have the same relationship as the two things in the first box.

1.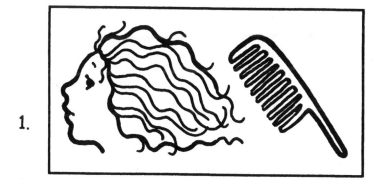

2.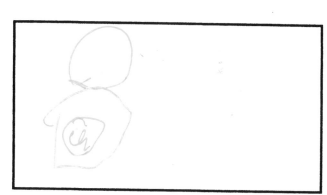

3.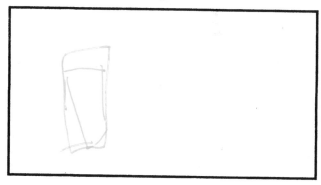

4.

Name _____

Cut out the pictures on page 25 and glue them in the second box so that these two things have the same relationship as the two things in the first box.

1.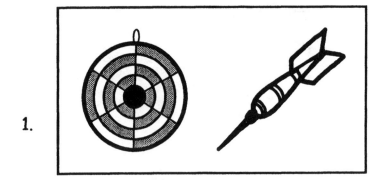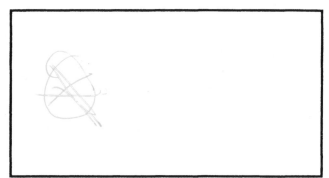

2.

3.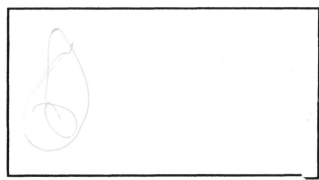

4.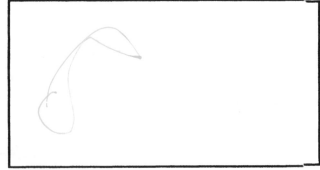

Name _____

Cut out the pictures on page 28 and glue them in the second box so that these two things have the same relationship as the two things in the first box.

1.

2.

3.

4.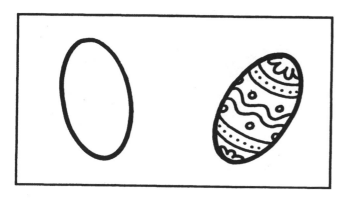

Lesson 21 Answer Blocks
Cut out these pictures. Use them to complete the analogies on page 26.

Lesson 22 Answer Blocks
Cut out these pictures. Use them to complete the analogies on page 27.

Name _____

Cut out the pictures on page 31 and glue them in the second box so that these two things have the same relationship as the two things in the first box.

1.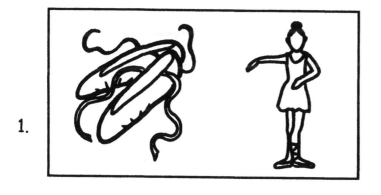

2.

3.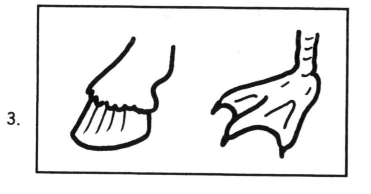

4.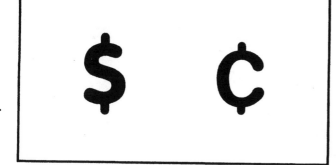

Name _____

Cut out the pictures on page 31 and glue them in the second box so that these two things have the same relationship as the two things in the first box.

1.

2.

3.

4.

Na _____

Cu __ t the pictures on page 37 and glue them in the second box so that these two
th ___ have the same relationship as the two things in the first box.

1.

2.

4.

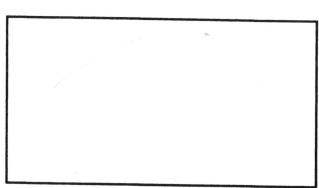

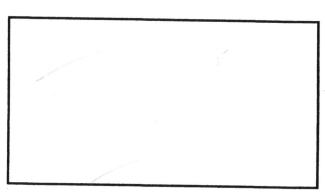

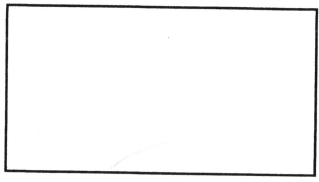

Name _____

Cut out the pictures on page 37 and glue them in the second box so that these two things have the same relationship as the two things in the first box.

1.

2.

3.

4.

Lesson 27 Answer Blocks

Cut out these pictures. Use them to complete the analogies on page 35.

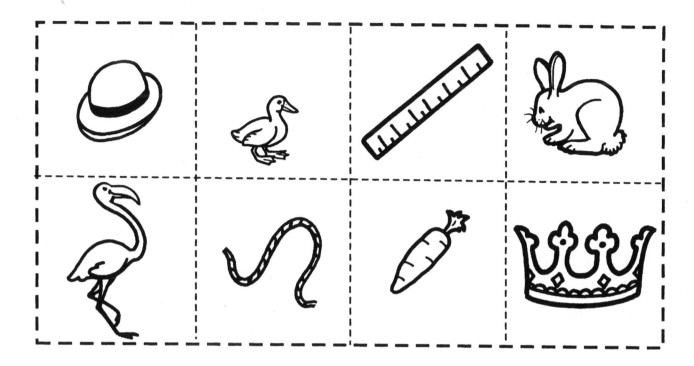

Lesson 28 Answer Blocks

Cut out these pictures. Use them to complete the analogies on page 36.

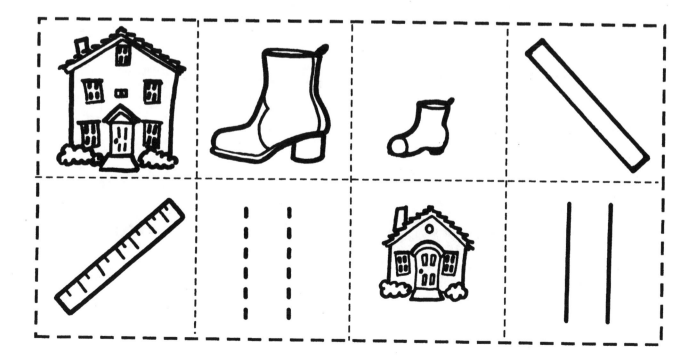

Name _____

Cut out the pictures on this page. Arrange the pictures to make four analogies. Glue the analogies on a large piece of paper.

Name _____

Cut out the pictures on this page. Arrange the pictures to make four analogies. Glue the analogies on a large piece of paper.

Name _____

Cut out the pictures on this page. Arrange the pictures to make four analogies. Glue the analogies on a large piece of paper.

Name _____

Cut out the pictures on this page. Arrange the pictures to make four analogies. Glue the analogies on a large piece of paper.

Name _____

Cut out the pictures on this page. Arrange the pictures to make four analogies. Glue the analogies on a large piece of paper.

Name _____

Cut out the pictures on this page. Arrange the pictures to make four analogies. Glue the analogies on a large piece of paper.

Name _____

Cut out the pictures on this page. Arrange the pictures to make four analogies. Glue the analogies on a large piece of paper.

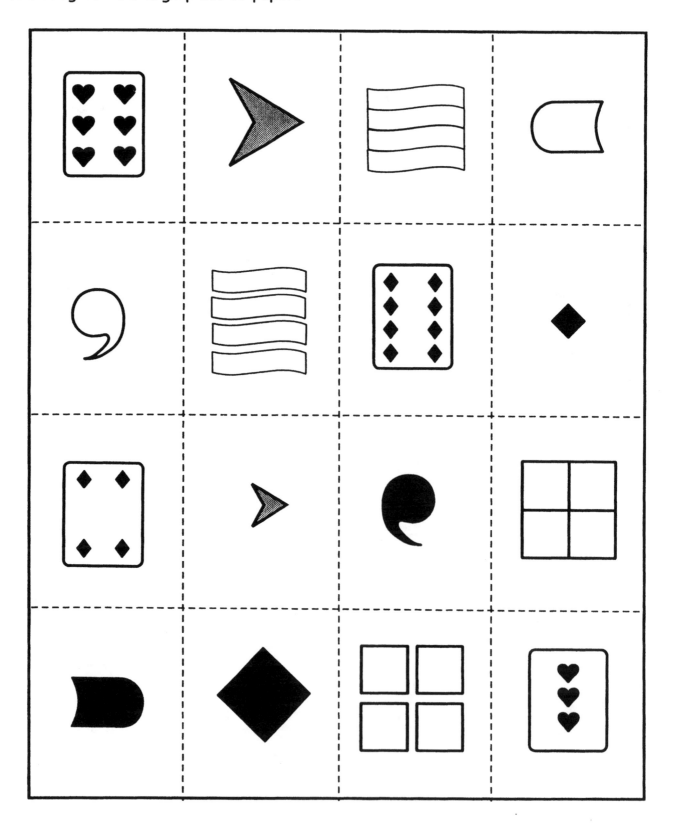

Name _____

Cut out the pictures on this page. Arrange the pictures to make four analogies. Glue the analogies on a large piece of paper.

Name _____

Cut out the pictures on this page. Arrange the pictures to make four analogies. Glue the analogies on a large piece of paper.

Answers

Lesson 1, *page 5*
1. cat - others are plants
2. frog -others are insects
3. bird - others live in the water
3. cheese - others are fruits or vegetables

Lesson 2, *page 6*
1. ball - others make noise
2. canoe - others have wheels
3. basketball hoop - you hit balls with the others
4. glue - others are things used to cut

Lesson 3, *page 7*
1. mittens - others are worn on the feet
2. wind surfer - others fly
3. apple - others are sweets
4. coat hanger - others are containers

Lesson 4, *page 8*
1. sandwich - others are things with which you eat
2. soda - others are types of sandwiches
3. helmet - others are hats
4. bee hive - others are places people live

Lesson 5, *page 9*
1. c. envelope
2. b. violin bow
3. a. clock
4. b. tooth
5. c. fish bowl

Lesson 6, *page 10*
1. a. paper
2. c. shirt
3. b. outlet
4. c. tennis ball
5. c. snowman

Lesson 7, *page 11*
1. b. jack-o'lantern
2. c. sock
3. a. nest
4. c. paint palette
5. b. chair

Lesson 8, *page 12*
1. b. dollar bill
2. a. umbrella
3. c. key
4. a lamp
5. c. eyes

Lesson 9, *page 13*
1. b
2. c
3. b
4. a
5. c

Lesson 10, *page 14*
1. b
2. a
3. c
4. a
5. a

Lesson 11, *page 15*
1. b
2. a
3. c
4. b
5. c

Lesson 12, *page 16*
1. b
2. c
3. c
4. a
5. b

Lesson 13, *page 17*
1. a
2. c
3. b
4. a
5. b

Lesson 14, *page 18*
1. c
2. a
3. b
4. b
5. a

Lesson 15, *page 19*
1. a
2. c
3. b
4. a
5. c

Lesson 16, *page 20*
1. a
2. b
3. c
4. a
5. a

Lesson 17, *page 21*
1. c
2. a
3. b
4. b
5. a

Lesson 18, *page 22*
1. c
2. b
3. c
4. a
5. c

Lesson 19, *page 23*
1. hair: comb :: tooth : toothbrush
2. bee : hive :: dog : doghouse
3. cup : glass :: stool : chair (order could be reversed)
4. carrot : rabbit :: banana : monkey

Lesson 20, *page 24*
1. dart board : dart :: bowling pin : bowling ball
2. single-story house : two-story house :: bed : bunk bed
3. wrench : bolt :: hammer : nail
4. dolphin : whale :: bird : ostrich

Lesson 21, *page 25*
1. peanuts : peanut butter :: milk : cheese
2. bow : violin :: drumstick : drum
3. cat : kitten :: boy : baby
4. spider : web :: bird : nest

Lesson 22, *page 27*
1. paint : brush :: peanut butter : knife
2. bike : motorcycle :: canoe : motor boat
3. apple : pie :: wheat : bread
4. egg : Easter egg :: tree : Christmas tree

Lesson 23, page 29
1. ballet shoes : ballerina :: ski boots : skier
2. tent : house :: lantern : lamp
3. hoof : web foot: horse : duck
4. dollar sign : cent sign :: dollar bill : coin

Lesson 24, page 30
1. ring : earring :: hand : ear

2.

3. spade : upside-down spade :: club : upside-down club
4. shield : decorated shield :: flag : decorated flag

Lesson 25, page 32

1.

2.

3.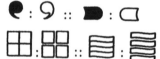

4.

Lesson 26, page 33
1. tomato : catsup :: peanuts :: peanut butter
2. screw : nail :: screwdriver : hammer
3. yarn : knitting needles :: fabric : sewing machine
4. 3 : tricycle :: 4 : wagon

Lesson 27, page 35
1. small flower : sunflower :: duck : flamingo
2. scale : flour :: ruler : rope
3. dog : bone :: rabbit : carrot
4. castle : house :: crown : hat

Lesson 28, page 36
1. single cone : double cone :: single-story house :: two-story house
2. circle : clock :: rectangle : ruler
3. dotted circle : solid circle :: dotted parallel line : solid parallel lines
4. big drum : small drum :: big boot : small boot

Note: Students may use a different order to form analogies in lessons 29-37. Check to make sure they have formed valid relationships and if so, accept their answers.

Lesson 29, page 38
sailboat : motorboat :: hot air balloon : airplane
baseball cap : baseball : helmet : football
sandwich : lunch box :: book(s) : backpack
toy : toy box :: book(s) : bookcase

Lesson 30, page 39
golf club : golf ball :: tennis racket : tennis ball
zipper : pants :: button : shirt
crayon : crayon box :: flower : bouquet of flowers
spoon : bowl :: shovel : pail

48

Lesson 31, page 40
soap : hand :: toothpaste : teeth
ice skates : roller-skates :: sled : wagon
syrup : pancakes :: catsup : hamburger
nose : flower :: eye : rainbow

Lesson 32, page 41
puzzle piece : puzzle :: brick : wall
hand : bell :: mouth : whistle
books : backpack :: clothes : suitcase

Lesson 33, page 42
coin : piggy bank :: envelope : mailbox
saw : log :: scissors : paper
January : snowman :: July : sand castle
caterpillar : butterfly :: tadpole : frog

Lesson 34, page 43

Lesson 35, page 44

Lesson 36, page 45

Lesson 37, page 46
piece of cake : whole cake :: piece of pizza : whole pizza

Name _____

Cut out the pictures on page 34 and glue them in the second box so that these two things have the same relationship as the two things in the first box.

1.

2.

3.

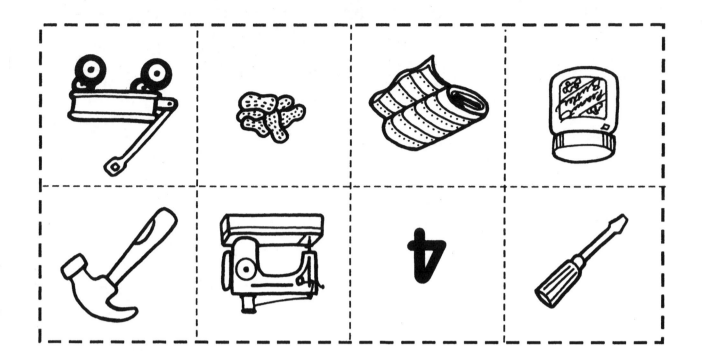

Cut out these pictures. Use them to complete the analogies on page 33.

Lesson 26 Answer Blocks

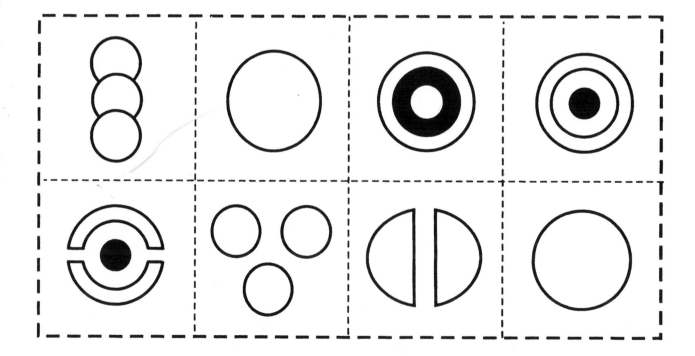

Cut out these pictures. Use them to complete the analogies on page 32.

Lesson 25 Answer Blocks